HOW THE WEST
WAS DRAWN
═ WOMEN'S ART ═

LINDA L. OSMUNDSON

PELICAN PUBLISHING COMPANY
GRETNA 2014

To the Burlington Northern Santa Fe Railway Company and Sally King, BNSF art curator, in appreciation of your support and generous contributions to this book and to the art education of children.

The word "Pelican" and the depiction of a pelican are trademarks of Pelican Publishing Company, Inc., and are registered in the U.S. Patent and Trademark Office.

Library of Congress Cataloging-in-Publication Data

Osmundson, Linda L.
  How the West was drawn : women's art / by Linda L. Osmundson.
      pages cm
  ISBN 978-1-4556-1878-1 (hardcover : alk. paper) 1. Women artists—West (U.S.)—Juvenile literature. 2. West (U.S.)—In art—Juvenile literature. I. Title.
  N8354.O86 2014
  704.9'49978—dc23

                                                            2013031683

Printed in Malaysia
Published by Pelican Publishing Company, Inc.
1000 Burmaster Street, Gretna, Louisiana 70053

INTRODUCTION

Few people realize how many American women painters worked in the West around the turn of the twentieth century. They are most often familiar with Georgia O'Keeffe. However, women have painted the West for more than 150 years. Since art was not an accepted career for women, they received little public attention. Some remained unknown because they didn't sign their works. Sometimes they used an alias, initials, or a form of their husband's name. They gifted their art to family. Relatives stored the works in boxes or trunks and hid them away in attics. Finding information about the women who painted the West is not easy.

Most women artists between 1850 and 1930 painted what society expected: still lifes, portraits, and landscapes. A few women strayed from those limitations and tackled sculpture. For the most part, Western women artists taught themselves. Lucky ones studied with Western artists such as Charles Russell and Frederic Remington. Some studied in such places as Chicago, the East Coast, and Europe.

San Francisco was one of the first western meeting places for women artists. The city grew after the discovery of gold in the nearby mountains. So did the women's artist population. Many women followed their husbands to the western frontier. In 1858, fifty women showed their art in a San Francisco art exhibit. Each year, more women contributed. Colorado's gold discoveries added another destination for Western women painters. They settled in Colorado Springs and Denver. Others joined art communities in New Mexico and Arizona.

Some women artists gained recognition when railroads began collecting Western art. The railroad companies hoped the art would attract travelers to the Southwest. The Santa Fe Railway purchased 108 paintings in 1903, many by women. Their collection hung in ticket offices, passenger stations, and Fred Harvey restaurants along travel routes. The women's paintings showed up on company literature, posters, and even in calendars.

The fourteen early women artists represented here are but a few who depicted the West. Today, women artists still paint the West. Thankfully, they face few of the problems these early women struggled to overcome.

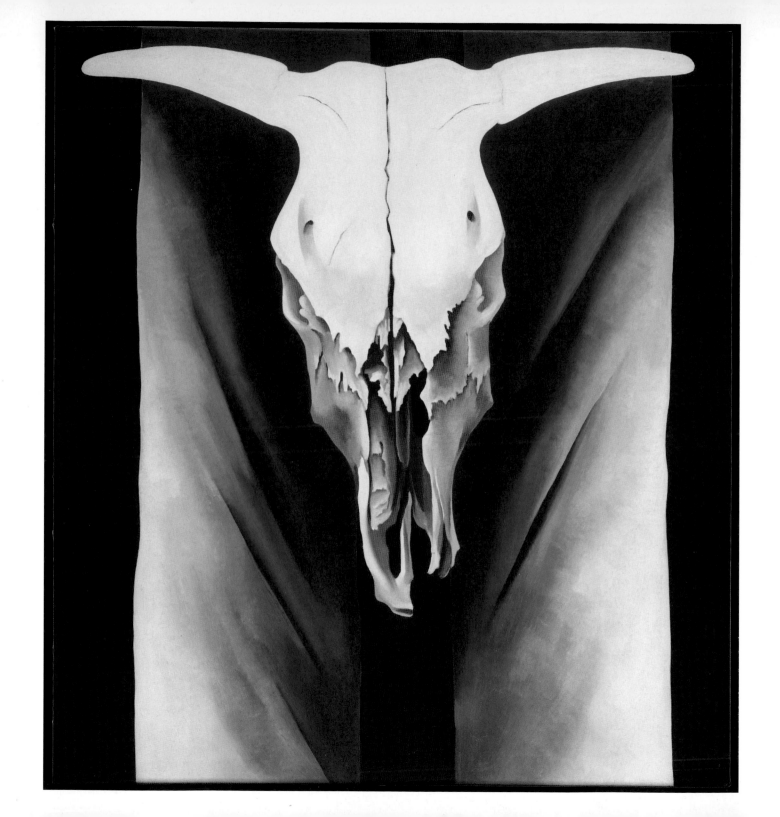

Name the colors you see.
What country do the three main colors represent?
Why would a skull stand for the West?
How does this work differ from others in the book?

Cows' skulls lay all over the West. Georgia O'Keeffe (1887-1986) painted this skull to show the undying spirit of America. She added the colors of America's flag: red, white, and blue.

O'Keeffe decided her artistic talents might never make her famous. She became a teacher. She continued to paint and study on the side. O'Keeffe searched for her own personal style. Lines, colors, shapes, and light and dark tones became her focus. More subjects included New York City buildings, landscapes, and close-up pictures of New Mexico's desert flowers.

O'Keeffe sent some charcoal drawings to a New York City friend. The friend shared the works with a well-known photographer and gallery owner. Alfred Stieglitz exhibited O'Keeffe's drawings without telling her. Everyone loved them. He asked her to give up teaching and move to New York City. He even offered to pay her way for a year. Years later, in 1924, O'Keeffe married Stieglitz, who was twenty-three years older than she.

Around 1929, O'Keeffe visited New Mexico's desert. After that, she returned for a few months out of every year. She spent a lot of quiet time alone in the wide open spaces. She painted the desert's big skies, colorful landscapes, flowers, and unusual buildings in a simple style of color and shape. After Stieglitz died, she moved to "O'Keeffe Country" permanently.

Before her death at age ninety-eight, Georgia O'Keeffe said, "I find that I have painted my life . . . without knowing."

Name everything you see in the
  painting, including colors.
What are the women doing?
How many pots are there?
What do the women wear on their
  feet?

In this picture, artist Alice Cleaver (1878?-1944) painted two Pueblo Indian women. One woman weaves on a backstrap loom. She attached one end of the loom to a pole. She pulled the vertical threads (warp) tight, connected them to a belt, and strapped the belt around her hips or back. Then the woman wove more threads (weft) horizontally. Several sticks held the threads tightly in place. This kind of loom made narrow objects such as belts. The girl watches and learns. They wear moccasins made from soft leather hide.

These women lived in groups of adobe houses called pueblos. Adobe is a mixture of clay, water, and something to hold the clay together (sticks, straw, or manure). The people who lived in those houses were named Pueblo Indians.

Cleaver studied art in Nebraska, Chicago, Pennsylvania, and Paris, France. Her parents insisted she come home from Paris. She lived with them for a while. Without her knowing, they hid letters from her boyfriend in their attic. Perhaps that is why she never married.

In 1907 and 1912, the Santa Fe Railway suggested she paint pictures of New Mexico and Arizona. Cleaver paid for the train tickets with her art. Her paintings showed the everyday life of the Pueblo and Pima Indians.

Cleaver won many awards for her works. Besides painting and teaching art, Alice Cleaver also taught violin.

Alice Cleaver
Pueblo Indian Weaver, 1912
Oil on canvas, 25" x 33"
Reprinted with permission of the BNSF Railway Company,
Fort Worth, Texas (AR-0159)

Why is the tree larger than the mountain?
What is reflected in the water?
How many people do you see?
What color are the shadows?
Are the artist's images outlined or fuzzy?

Jessie Benton Evans (1866-1954) painted the mountain smaller than the tree. It created a feeling of three dimensions. She highlighted the red color where the sun shone on the rocky mountainside. She mirrored the same color for the reflection in the water.

Evans used an Impressionistic painting style. She painted shadows purple instead of black. She did not outline her objects but made the images fuzzy. The picture becomes clearer when viewed from farther away.

Although Evans was born in Ohio, she studied art in Chicago. She married a man who encouraged her artistic dreams. She took their only son to Europe to see the sights while she studied art.

Because of her poor health, the Evans family moved to Phoenix, Arizona. They built a home that looked like an Italian house. At first, she did not like the hot, dry desert. Over time, she learned to love its many colors. She used them in her landscapes. The wide-open desert gave her a feeling of never-ending time.

People dubbed her "Madame Evans." She invited artists, sculptors, actors, writers, and musicians to her home. When her son grew up, he built hotels. They sold Evans's paintings. The Santa Fe Railway bought thirteen works by Evans, more than those of any other woman artist.

The people of Arizona called Evans one of the state's most outstanding artists.

Jessie Benton Evans
Granite Mountain near Phoenix, 1917
Oil on canvas, 24" x 30"
Reprinted with permission of the BNSF Railway Company, Fort Worth, Texas (AR-0268)

What is the title of this sculpture?
Where are the cowboys headed?
How do you know they are in a
  hurry?
Find the cowboy with wooly chaps.
Which cowboy is not looking
  where he is going?

Sally James Farnham (1869-1943) sculpted this piece, *Payday,* to look like *Coming Thru the Rye* by her friend Frederic Remington. One cowboy leans forward in his hurry to get to town and spend his pay. Another urges his horse with a rope. A third ducks his head to shield his face from the wind. The horses look to be in a full gallop.

Farnham became sick and had to stay in bed for many months. Her husband gave her plasticine, a substitute for wax or clay, to keep her from being bored. She shaped small figures. Sculpting felt natural. She believed her fingers and thumbs knew what to do.

By the time Farnham turned thirty-nine, word of her impressive sculptures spread. She sculpted the heads of two presidents: Theodore Roosevelt and Warren G. Harding. She made reliefs, trophies, heads, and huge monuments. She won a contest and made the largest piece (fifteen feet high) ever sculpted by a woman of that time. Installed in 1921, the Simon Bolivar statue stands in New York City's Central Park.

Los Angeles hired her to make a sixteen-foot copy of *Payday.* For some reason, it was never completed. Between 1930 and 1938, she cast three more copies from the original. Farnham wrote to a friend that she "considers it one of her best works."

Sally James Farnham
Payday, 1930
Bronze, 18" x 23" x 18"
Woolaroc Museum, Bartlesville, Oklahoma (SCT-14)

Name the colors you see.
Do you think this is a boy or girl?
Why is the dog watching the
  child?
What do you think the basket
  held?
Find a fire.

Yokia Treasures is one of the largest of Grace Carpenter Hudson's (1865-1937) lifelike oil paintings. Rather than cowboys or frontiersmen, she most often painted Pomo Indian men, women, and children. Here, she shows three things a Pomo Indian treasured: a child, basket, and dog. The dog waits for the boy to drop scraps.

The Pomos were known for their beautiful basket weaving. Weavers wove their famous baskets so tightly, they served as infant carriers. Hudson included this large basket, which stored acorns, in her painting.

Grace and her twin brother, Grant, grew up with and around these wonderful Pomo people. They gladly posed for her. She painted more than six hundred Pomo portraits.

After Hudson's death, a museum was built behind her home and studio in Ukiah, California. The museum houses her art and historic documents. It also displays a collection of Pomo artifacts.

A magazine of her time wrote that San Franciscans loved Hudson's art: "A canvas from her brush is sold before it leaves the easel." Her paintings filled an empty space in Western art by presenting her loving view of Pomo culture.

Hudson said, "My desire is that the world shall know them as I know them, and before they vanish."

Grace Carpenter Hudson
Yokia Treasures, 1894
Oil on canvas, 38" x 30"
Courtesy of the Grace Hudson Museum and Sun House,
Ukiah, California (2006-11-1)

Name the colors you see.
How many people are in the picture?
What is the Indian woman doing?
How is the beehive structure used?

Blanche Dugan Cole's (1868-1956) loose brush strokes depict an Indian woman baking bread in an adobe oven called a *horno*. Her oil-paint palette includes earthy browns and reds, the colors of the Arizona desert. Like this picture, her small paintings measured slightly larger than a piece of notebook paper.

Although born in Indiana, Cole moved with her parents to Leadville, Colorado, when she was young. Her father, a doctor, provided the medical needs of the gold and silver miners. She gained her first fame through writing instead of art. In 1886, she wrote several articles for the *Leadville (CO) Herald Democrat* about her travels.

Blanche Cole studied art in Italy, Spain, and France. Her paintings hung in many European exhibits. When she came home, she traveled back and forth between Leadville and Denver. She married William Cole, an artist and businessman.

Cole taught art classes in Denver. A new job sent her to northern Arizona to paint. From then on, Cole's career took a different path: Western art and Indians. The Santa Fe Railroad purchased eight of Cole's paintings.

After she and her husband moved to Los Angeles, Cole continued to write and teach. She often illustrated her own articles. Even though she lived for a long time in Colorado, it is believed that she never painted the Rocky Mountains.

Blanche Dugan Cole
Southwestern Scene, 1907
Oil on canvas, 13½" x 9½"
Reprinted with permission of the BNSF Railway Company, Fort Worth, Texas (AR-1069)

What is the Indian woman doing? How does she use the blue bowl? The pottery has no designs. Why? How does the artist show a shiny surface?

Grace May Betts (1883-1978) painted this famous Pueblo potter, Maria Martinez. Although she had only seen Martinez in black and white photographs, Betts painted the famous potter in colorful clothing. Notice the patterned dress, fringed shawl, and turquoise jewelry. The Indian woman sits in front of a dull, cracked adobe wall. She works on several of her famous black pots.

The pots are plain. Martinez's husband added the designs to her pots later. To make her pottery, Martinez smoothed snake-like coils into a shape. She brushed it with slip (watery clay) from the blue bowl. Martinez polished the unfired shape with a stone. Betts added spots of white to the pots to represent a shiny surface.

Betts's parents, sister, and three brothers were artists. First, she studied with her father. Later, she attended school at the Art Institute of Chicago. Betts painted mostly landscapes until the 1940s. Then, she changed her subjects to Indians. Betts purchased a house trailer and drove all over the Southwest. She lived and worked in her mobile studio.

The Santa Fe Railroad bought five of Betts's paintings. They paid her an amount almost equal to what they paid men. The city of San Francisco hired Betts to paint the backdrops for animal displays in Golden Gate Park. She also illustrated magazine articles and children's books.

Grace May Betts
Maria Martinez, 1951
Oil on canvas, 36" x 48"
Reprinted with permission of the BNSF Railway Company,
Fort Worth, Texas (AR-0066)

What are these houses called?

How many house levels do you see?

How do the people get from one floor to the next?

What bird do the dancers represent?

Edith Hamlin Dixon (1902-92) portrayed the Eagle Dance in this mural. Two young men wore eagle costumes over their yellow-painted bodies. They spread their wings and mimicked the bird's flight. When she lived in Taos, New Mexico, some Indians performed the dance in her living room.

The Indians lived in adobe houses. The houses rose at least five stories from the ground. People climbed ladders to get from one floor to the next. In this painting, two men dance outside of the old Taos Pueblo. People still live in the pueblo today.

Dixon painted many large murals. This one is taller than most bedroom walls and almost as wide as an average elementary-school classroom. She added shadows to give a three-dimensional feeling. This mural hung in three locations before it settled in the office of the Burlington Northern Santa Fe Railway in Fort Worth, Texas.

In San Francisco, Edith Hamlin painted murals in Coit Tower and Mission High School. Maynard Dixon, a well-known artist, advised her. He was twenty-seven years older than she. They married in 1937. Her husband called her "Speedy Edie." Her stepsons said she "whooped with laughter and bounced with energy." They said she never looked where she was going when she drove a car.

The Dixons moved to Tucson, Arizona, for the winters and Maynard's health. They spent summers in a log house in Mt. Carmel, Utah. After his death in 1946, she left the Southwest and returned to San Francisco.

Edith Hamlin Dixon
Pueblo-Eagle Dance Mural: The Eagle Dance at Taos, 1946
Oil on canvas, 9'4" x 17'5"
Reprinted with permission of the BNSF Railway Company, Fort Worth, Texas (AR-0216)

What animal does the chief's headdress represent?
What is he doing?
How was a peace pipe used?
How did he decorate his face?

Kathryn Leighton (1875-1952) loved to paint portraits. This one shows a Blood Indian chief in a buffalo headdress made with eagle feathers. She added a lightning bolt design to his face. To make a peace pipe, the chief attached a red pipestone bowl to a long, hollow, wooden stick. Indians painted their faces and smoked sacred pipes for religious ceremonies and to seal promises. The peace pipe could be used to decide if a man were honest.

Kathryn Leighton stepped into a man's art world. She painted about seven hundred Indian portraits. She invited the Indians to her studio, where they danced, whooped, and played drums. Sometimes, she hired actors as models instead of real Indians.

American West painter and sculptor Charles Russell introduced Leighton to Blackfoot leaders and Great Northern Railway executives. The railway hired her to paint portraits of the Blackfoot, who lived in Glacier National Park. Her paintings recorded Indian clothing, homes, and traditions. The railway purchased twenty of her paintings. They sent the pictures with an Indian-culture expert on a cross-country tour. The Blackfoot adopted Leighton and called her Anna-Tar-Kee. It means "beautiful woman in spirit."

Leighton said of her portraits, "I am trying to put on canvas the nobility of the old Indian as I see him, the beauty of the colour, the dignity of tradition and the fundamental beliefs of our first American people. . . ."

Kathryn Leighton
A Blood Chief (Canadian)
Oil, 44" x 36"
Gilcrease Museum, Tulsa, Oklahoma (0137.1870)

Is this a man or a woman?
Is this sculpture made out of
   wood, stone, or bronze?
Would you like to meet this
   person?
Why or why not?

Malvina Hoffman (1885-1966) photo-graphed this Apache man at an Indian boarding school. She later sculpted him in a soft artist's clay, took it to a foundry, and made it into bronze. A frown puckers his forehead. No smile creases his cheeks or eyes. He reveals no feelings—happy or sad, kind or cruel. Yet, he looks real. If an Apache Indian viewed this sculpture, he would recognize the man as a cultural brother.

Hoffman's father taught her to observe people. She also dissected human bodies to learn about bones and muscles. Those lessons trained her to portray lifelike people.

Malvina Hoffman performed all the jobs necessary to make her sculptures. She sharpened and cleaned her own tools, lifted heavy equipment, bent iron, and sawed wood. She learned to carve wood, stone, and marble. At the foundry, she watched workers turn her clay figures into bronze sculptures. Occasionally, she climbed on top of figures as tall as giraffes. Her hard work often left her tired and sick.

The Chicago Field Museum asked Hoffman to sculpt every ethnic group on Earth. For eight months, she traveled all over the world. She said that it took "five years" of study and work to complete the collection of 101 sculptures for the museum's Hall of Man. She created busts like this and full-sized figures. She sculpted American Indians last.

Hoffman died at the age of eighty-one. A New York newspaper called her "one of the few women to reach first rank as a sculptor . . ."

Malvina Hoffman
Jicarilla Apache, 1934
Bronze, Life-size
Courtesy the Field Museum, Chicago, Illinois (MH65)

Are these cowboys or Indians?
How are they dressed?
What are they doing?
What do you think will happen next?

Marjorie Holmes Thomas (1885-1978) copied the Impressionists' style in her use of colors such as the purple instead of black shadows. She used few harsh lines.

These Indian braves are dressed more like cowboys than Indians. The men wear no beads, leather shirts, or feathers. They wear cowboy pants and cotton shirts. A brimmed hat covers their head and bandanas drape their necks. Each man carries a rope in case the bronco rider needs help. They do not ride bareback, but sit upon saddles, their feet in stirrups.

When Thomas's brother became ill, she gave up her East Coast home and art schools. She moved with him and their mother to the drier climate of Arizona. In the new location, she chose to paint animals rather than the portraits she crafted in the east.

Thomas preferred to depict daily activities. She painted the Indians while they tried to break, or tame, their horses. The rider saddled the horse, climbed aboard, and rode until the horse relaxed and accepted him on its back. In other pictures, she drew the mule teams that dredged Arizona's Salt River Canal.

Like many people during the Great Depression of the 1930s, artists needed jobs. The government formed the Public Works of Art Project. It hired artists to paint murals or smaller pictures in government buildings. Thomas's paintings hung in the Arizona governor's executive office.

Even after her brother died, Thomas continued to call Arizona home.

Marjorie Holmes Thomas
Indians Breaking Bronco, 1913
Oil on canvas, 22" x 28"
Reprinted with permission of the BNSF Railway Company,
Fort Worth, Texas (AR-0761)

How old do you think this girl is?
What makes her hair style
  unusual?
What is in the basket on the left?
How did the artist sign this image?

Lydia Dunham Smith Fabian (1857-1947) displayed thirty-four pieces of art in 1923. She said that every picture told a story. Yet, most of her life's story is missing.

Supposedly, she loved to paint portraits. This one tells the story of a teenage Hopi girl. Young women seldom wore this hairstyle by the time Fabian painted the portrait. Perhaps the artist wished to tell a story that included past Hopi customs. The style of two side circles of hair meant the Hopi girl was not married. The girl weaves a plaque, one job of Hopi women. A basket of reeds sits to her right ready for use. No design plan appeared on paper. The weaver worked from a pattern in her head. Fabian illustrates Indian symbols woven into the basket, plaques, and rug.

Even though little information exists about Fabian, researchers discovered she studied at ten different United States art schools. She traveled the world as a young woman. When she was thirty-three years old, her father died. From his obituary, historians learned she had married Lincoln Smith, a department store salesman. He died in 1900. She married Ernst Fabian in 1915.

During her lifetime, she taught art classes at a college in Illinois. She added photography to her list of accomplishments. If researchers find other Lydia Fabian paintings and photographs, more of her life story could be revealed.

Lydia Dunham Smith Fabian
Hopi Girl with Plaque, 1917
Oil on canvas, 24" x 20"
Reprinted with permission of the BNSF Railway Company, Fort Worth, Texas (AR-0272)

What do you see first?
Who are the people?
Why does the picture look two-dimensional?

Catharine Carter Critcher (1868-1964) combines a portrait and a still life in *Pueblo Family*. The still-life flowers and their bright, happy colors draw your attention first. The handmade pot and flowers almost hide the Pueblo couple. The picture looks flat because there are no shadows to create depth.

Critcher grew up on a Virginia plantation. Her wealthy parents encouraged her love of drawing. She studied art in New York and Washington, DC. She painted portraits, figures, landscapes, and still lifes. Critcher also studied in Paris. While there, she opened a school to teach American art students the language and how to be accepted into French art schools.

Upon her return to Washington, DC, Critcher taught in an art school for six years. Eventually, she and a friend started the Critcher School of Painting and Applied Arts. She ran the school until it closed in 1940 and she became a full-time artist.

On a visit to Taos, New Mexico, Critcher fell in love with the area and native people. She wrote to a friend, "Taos is unlike any place God ever made . . . There are models galore and no phones." She spent many summers working outdoors in New Mexico. The sun tanned and wrinkled her skin.

The men in the Taos Society of Artists welcomed Critcher as a member in 1924. She was the only woman accepted into the all-male organization.

Catharine Carter Critcher
Pueblo Family, 1928
Oil on canvas, 30" x 30½"
Courtesy of the Eiteljorg Museum of American Indians and Western Art, Indianapolis, Indiana

Is this picture drawn with soft or hard lines?

How would it feel to ride in a stagecoach over this trail?

How many white horses can you find?

What time of year is it?

Marjorie Reed (1915-96) is best known for her paintings of the Butterfield Overland Stage coaches. *Old Santa Paula Stage* was her first stagecoach picture. She loved to paint horses. Each team of four to six horses usually included one white horse. She used Impressionist techniques of soft lines rather than hard ones. Look at the picture from farther away, and see how the colors blend together and form unlined images. Notice the bare canvas that outlines the clouds.

Old stagecoach trips took a long time. For instance, a two thousand-mile trip from Missouri to San Francisco required about twenty-four days. Today, the same distance can be driven in three or four days. Reed paints a stagecoach tossed along a typical rough, rocky trail. Up to six passengers rode on benches in a space equal to the inside of a small car. Reed illustrates how the luggage and mail bags were carried.

Reed first studied art with her father. In her lifetime, she supposedly created about ten thousand works of art. At one time, she signed her paintings Harvey Day, the name of one of her four husbands.

As a teenager, Reed worked for Walt Disney. She quit because she preferred to paint outside rather than inside. After she found a stray dog, he rode along in the car on her many sketching and painting trips. Because she said "Oh, boy," every time he caused trouble, she named him Boy.

Marjorie Reed declared she "never painted anything. I just held the brush and God did the work."

Marjorie Reed
Old Santa Paula Stage, ca. 1938
Oil on canvas, 20" x 24"
Courtesy of Gary Fillmore, Blue Coyote Gallery, Cave Creek, Arizona

DID YOU KNOW THESE FASCINATING FACTS?

More than one thousand women artists painted the West beginning in 1843. One of the first was Eliza Griffin Johnston (1821-96).

San Francisco served as the first art hub for women of the American West.

In the 1850s, women artists sailed from the East Coast to San Francisco. Sometimes, they sailed on ships from the Atlantic Ocean to the Pacific Ocean around the southern tip of South America. Other times, they cruised to Panama and traveled about thirty miles on land across the Isthmus of Panama. Then they boarded another ship on its way to California.

Beginning in the late 1850s, stagecoaches trekked from the end of railroad lines into California. Women rode with as many as eighteen passengers. Nine rode inside and nine rode on top—with no seatbelts.

Frances Flora ("Fanny") Palmer (1812-76) was well known for her Western paintings. However, she never traveled west of New Jersey.

Western women artists improved their art by taking classes. In 1874, a San Francisco class signed up sixty students. Forty-six of them were women.

At a San Francisco exhibition of women artists, there were 270 pieces of art by eighty-one women. After that, women were no longer called "Sunday painters."

Women artists also traveled to Colorado. Most lived in Denver and Colorado Springs. Helen Henderson Chain (1849-92) painted the Rocky Mountains and other Western locations. Alice Cooper (1875-1937) created a life-sized sculpture of Sacajawea. It was displayed at the 1905 Lewis and Clark Centennial Exposition, where everyone would see it.

William Simpson, chief of advertising of the Santa Fe Railway, bought thirty-five canvases of women's art around 1903. Besides those in this book, he bought works by Marion Kavanaugh Wachtel (1870-1954), Ethel Louise Coe (1878-1938), and Nellie Ellen Shepherd (1877-1920).

A brochure was handed out at the 1904 Louisiana Purchase Exposition in St. Louis, Missouri. It included twenty-one pictures by Abby William Hill (1861-1943). More than thirty-thousand people saw the brochures.

Sculptures and murals created in the 1930s by Western artists can still be found in many post offices and government buildings. Locations with paintings by women include cities in Colorado, Arizona, Montana, Idaho, Utah, Oklahoma, and California.

Can you find works by women in your city's government buildings?
What other fascinating facts about women artists can you discover?